THIS BOOK
holds the prayerful
thoughts of:

_____

_____

Kindness, when given away,
keeps coming back.

The dearest things of life are mostly near at hand.

For the law of the Spirit of life in Christ Jesus
hath made me free from the law of sin and death.

—ROMANS 8:2

It is better to hold out a helping hand than
to point a finger.

Jesus answered,
"My kingdom is not of this world: if my kingdom
were of this world, then would my servants fight,
that I should not be delivered to the Jews: but
now is my kingdom not from hence."

—JOHN 18:36

Be what you wish others to become.

Let your conversation be without covetousness;
and be content with such things as ye have: for he
hath said, "I will never leave thee, nor forsake thee."

—Hebrews 13:5

Good intentions spoil if not used.

In like manner also, that women adorn
themselves in modest apparel, with
shamefacedness and sobriety; not with broided
hair, or gold, or pearls, or costly array.

—1 Timothy 2:9

Every man must live with the man
he makes of himself.

Blessed are the pure in heart:
for they shall see God.

—Matthew 5:8

If you must doubt, doubt your doubts,
not your beliefs.

A fool uttereth all his mind: but a wise man
keepeth it in till afterwards.

—PROVERBS 29:11

It is better to suffer wrong than to
commit wrong.

Rest in the LORD, and wait patiently for him:
fret not thyself because of him who prospereth
in his way, because of the man who bringeth
wicked devices to pass.

—PSALM 37:7

Judge a man by his questions, not by his answers.

And be ye kind one to another, tenderhearted,
forgiving one another, even as God for Christ's
sake hath forgiven you.

—EPHESIANS 4:32

Live each short hour with God, and the long
years will take care of themselves.

And the multitude of them that believed were
of one heart and of one soul: neither said any of
them that ought of the things which he possessed
was his own; but they had all things common.

—Acts 4:32

Peace is seeing a sunset and knowing
who to thank.

Every word of God is pure: he is a shield unto
them that put their trust in him.

—Proverbs 30:5

No joy is complete unless it is shared.

But ye are a chosen generation, a royal priesthood, an holy nation, a peculiar people; that ye should shew forth the praises of him who hath called you out of darkness into his marvellous light.

—1 Peter 2:9

Teaching children to count is fine, but teaching
them what counts is better.

_____

_____

_____

_____

_____

_____

_____

_____

_____

_____

_____

_____

_____

_____

_____

_____

_____

_____

_____

_____

_____

Ye have heard that it hath been said, An eye for an
eye, and a tooth for a tooth: But I say unto you,
That ye resist not evil: but whosoever shall smite
thee on thy right cheek, turn to him the other also.

—MATTHEW 5:38–39

You only live once, but if you work it right,
once is enough.

I am the vine, ye are the branches: He that abideth
in me, and I in him, the same bringeth forth much
fruit: for without me ye can do nothing.

—John 15:5

To grow old gracefully,
you must start when you are young.

_____

_____

_____

_____

_____

_____

_____

_____

_____

_____

_____

_____

_____

_____

_____

_____

_____

_____

_____

_____

_____

_____

_____

Therefore I say unto you, Take no thought for your
life, what ye shall eat, or what ye shall drink; nor
yet for your body, what ye shall put on. Is not the
life more than meat, and the body than raiment?

—Matthew 6:25

The person who kills time has not
learned the value of life.

And God blessed the seventh day, and sanctified it: because that in it he had rested from all his work which God created and made.

—GENESIS 2:3

A man is never old until his regrets
outnumber his dreams.

Now therefore, if ye will obey my voice indeed, and keep my covenant, then ye shall be a peculiar treasure unto me above all people: for all the earth is mine.

—Exodus 19:5

We don't realize how wonderful today
is until tomorrow.

Train up a child in the way he should go: and
when he is old, he will not depart from it.

—PROVERBS 22:6

Worse than failure is the failure to try.

For we walk by faith, not by sight.

—2 CORINTHIANS 5:7

Don't call the world dirty because you've
forgotten to clean your windows.

For other foundation can no man lay than that is
laid, which is Jesus Christ.

—1 CORINTHIANS 3:11

Experience is the great teacher.

Lay not up for yourselves treasures upon earth, where moth and rust doth corrupt, and where thieves break through and steal: But lay up for yourselves treasures in heaven, where neither moth nor rust doth corrupt, and where thieves do not break through nor steal: For where your treasure is, there will your heart be also.

—MATTHEW 6:19–21

You will always leave something behind:
your influence.

And be not conformed to this world: but be ye transformed by the renewing of your mind, that ye may prove what is that good, and acceptable, and perfect, will of God.

—ROMANS 12:2

A handful of patience is worth more
than a bushel of brains.

The thief cometh not, but for to steal, and to kill, and to destroy: I am come that they might have life, and that they might have it more abundantly.

—JOHN 10:10

You begin to slip when you'd rather win an
argument than be right.

Turn away mine eyes from beholding vanity; and
quicken thou me in thy way.

—Psalm 119:37

An ounce of work is worth a ton of wishing.

Then Peter and the other apostles answered and said, "We ought to obey God rather than men."

—ACTS 5:29

Anyone who practices what he preaches doesn't
have to preach much.

Wealth gotten by vanity shall be diminished: but
he that gathereth by labour shall increase.

—PROVERBS 13:11

Being human is a privilege, not an excuse.

For if ye forgive men their trespasses, your
heavenly Father will also forgive you.

—MATTHEW 6:14

Beware of the man who knows the answer before
he understands the question.

And when ye stand praying, forgive, if ye have
ought against any: that your Father also which is
in heaven may forgive you your trespasses.

—MARK 11:25

A great deal of what we see depends
on what we are looking for.

And God Almighty bless thee, and make
thee fruitful, and multiply thee, that thou
mayest be a multitude of people.

—GENESIS 28:3

Kindness, when given away, keeps coming back.

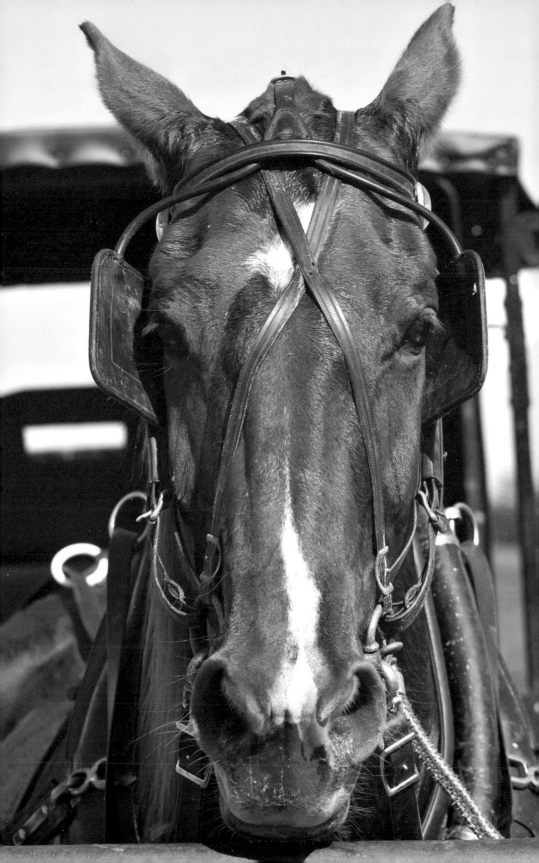

Love not the world, neither the things that are in the world. If any man love the world, the love of the Father is not in him.

—1 JOHN 2:15

The more you know, the more you
know you don't know.

Envy thou not the oppressor, and choose
none of his ways.

—Proverbs 3:31

It takes both rain and sunshine to make
the garden grow.

_____

_____

_____

_____

_____

_____

_____

_____

_____

_____

_____

_____

_____

_____

_____

_____

_____

_____

_____

_____

Thou shalt not make unto thee any graven image,
or any likeness of any thing that is in heaven
above, or that is in the earth beneath, or that is
in the water under the earth.

—Exodus 20:4

There's a difference between good, sound reasons
and reasons that sound good.

Pure religion and undefiled before God and
the Father is this, To visit the fatherless and
widows in their affliction, and to keep himself
unspotted from the world.

—JAMES 1:27

Harvest comes not every day.

Be ye not unequally yoked together with unbelievers: for what fellowship hath righteousness with unrighteousness? and what communion hath light with darkness?

—2 Corinthians 6:14

Don't pull up your garden to see if it's growing.

Blessed are the merciful:
for they shall obtain mercy.

—MATTHEW 5:7

What other people think of you is none
of your business.

Peace I leave with you, my peace I give unto you:
not as the world giveth, give I unto you. Let not
your heart be troubled, neither let it be afraid.

—JOHN 14:27

Good deeds have echoes.

ISBN 978-1-64178-028-5

© 2018 by Quiet Fox Designs, *www.QuietFoxDesigns.com*, an imprint of Fox Chapel Publishing Company, Inc., 903 Square Street, Mount Joy, PA 17552.

Scripture quotations are from the King James Version of the Bible.

Shutterstock credits: A. L. Spangler (131); Bob Pool (144); Christian Kieffer (83); Dan Thornberg (98); Delmas Lehman (2); Denise Kappa (115); Derek Gordon (20); FernandoH (67); hutch photography (front cover photo); Michael G McKinne (35); Vladislav Gajic (50)
Patterns on front cover, back cover, and endpapers: Justin Speers

We are always looking for talented authors and artists. To submit an idea, please send a brief inquiry to acquisitions@foxchapelpublishing.com.

Fox Chapel Publishing makes every effort to use environmentally friendly paper for printing.

Printed in China

First printing